• MEET •
HENRI ROUSSEAU

Read With You Center for Excellence in STEAM Education

Read With You

Myself: Portrait, 1890

The Eiffel Tower, c. 1898

Outskirts of Paris, c. 1897-1905

Tropical Forest with Monkeys, 1910

A Centennial of Independence, 1892

Portrait of a Woman in a Landscape, c. 1893–1896

Surprised!, 1891

The Sleeping Traveler, 1897

Find Examples

This painting is titled *Seine and Eiffel Tower in the Sunset* (1896–1898).

What colors can you see in the water? Where do those colors come from?

Are the leaves orange because of the sunset or the season? Why do you think so?

How are the buildings in the picture painted differently from the plants? Look closely at the brushstrokes.

Connect

This painting is titled *Woman Walking in an Exotic Forest* (1905).

Which plants look flat in this painting? What makes them look flat?

What is the woman wearing in this painting? Are they the best clothes for walking in a forest?

Have you ever imagined you were on a mountain or in a jungle? What did the place look like?

Think of five plants or buildings that could be in your imaginary place.

Craft

Option 1

1. Go outside to a park or forest.

2. Take close-up pictures of several kinds of leaves and wildflowers.

3. At home, look at your photos and draw a picture with all the leaves and flowers in it.

Option 2

1. Think of a far-off mountain, jungle, forest, or desert you want to visit.

2. Draw a picture of yourself in that place, copying the style of Rousseau's artworks.

3. Just like Rousseau, sign your artwork boldly in the bottom left or right corner.

Made in the USA
Las Vegas, NV
19 January 2024